A Note to Parents

DK READERS is a compelling program for beginning readers, designed in conjunction with leading literacy experts, including Dr. Linda Gambrell, Distinguished Professor of Education at Clemson University. Dr. Gambrell has served as President of the National Reading Conference, the College Reading Association, and the International Reading Association.

Beautiful illustrations and superb full-color photographs combine with engaging, easy-to-read stories to offer a fresh approach to each subject in the series. Each DK READER is guaranteed to capture a child's interest while developing his or her reading skills, general knowledge, and love of reading.

The five levels of DK READERS are aimed at different reading abilities, enabling you to choose the books that are exactly right for your child:

Pre-level 1: Learning to read
Level 1: Beginning to read
Level 2: Beginning to read alone
Level 3: Reading alone
Level 4: Proficient readers

The "normal" age at which a child begins to read can be anywhere from three to eight years old. Adult participation through the lower levels is very helpful for providing encouragement, discussing storylines, and sounding out unfamiliar words.

No matter which level you select, you can be sure that you are helping your child learn to read, then read to learn!

DK

LONDON, NEW YORK, MUNICH,
MELBOURNE, AND DELHI

Senior Editor Helen Murray
Designer Lauren Rosier
Managing Editor Laura Gilbert
Design Manager Nathan Martin
Publishing Manager Julie Ferris
Art Director Ron Stobbart
Publishing Director Simon Beecroft
Pre-Production Producer Rebecca Fallowfield
Producer Louise Daly

Designed and edited by Tall Tree Ltd
Designer Richard Horsford
Editor Catherine Saunders

Reading Consultant
Linda B. Gambrell, Ph.D.

First American Edition, 2013
10 9 8 7 6 5 4 3 2 1
Published in the United States by DK Publishing
375 Hudson Street, New York, New York 10014

001–187437–March/13

Published in Great Britain by Dorling Kindersley Limited

DK books are available at special discounts when purchased in bulk for sales promotions, premiums, fund-raising, or educational use.
For details, contact:
DK Publishing Special Markets
375 Hudson Street, New York, New York 10014
SpecialSales@dk.com

A catalog record for this book is available from the Library of Congress.

ISBN: 978-1-4654-0259-2 (paperback)
ISBN: 978-1-4654-0260-8 (hardback)

Color reproduction by Alta Image
Printed and bound in China by L.Rex

Discover more at
www.dk.com
www.LEGO.com

Contents

Pallavee chelavaada

READING 3 ALONE

Summer Adventures

Written by Catherine Saunders

Summer's here!

It's summertime in Heartlake City. With no school for a few weeks, Mia, Olivia, Stephanie, Andrea, and Emma can enjoy the sunshine. Each girl has some great ideas for summer fun.

Olivia is busy planning her amazing summer! What should she do first?

Andrea, Stephanie, Emma, Mia, and Olivia are looking forward to their summer vacations. They've all got some very exciting adventures planned.

Turn the page to find out who will be making sweet music, who is planning a trip, and who will be working hard. Discover who is off to riding camp, who will be taking to the skies, and, most importantly, what the girls will be doing together.

There's something exciting to suit everyone, so come and join the girls on their fantastic summer adventures.

Up, up, and away!

Stephanie thinks the best place to have a summer adventure is in the sky. She has a special type of plane that can take off and land on water. It's called a seaplane. Stephanie has been taking flying lessons at the Heartlake Flying Club for a few months. She's a natural!

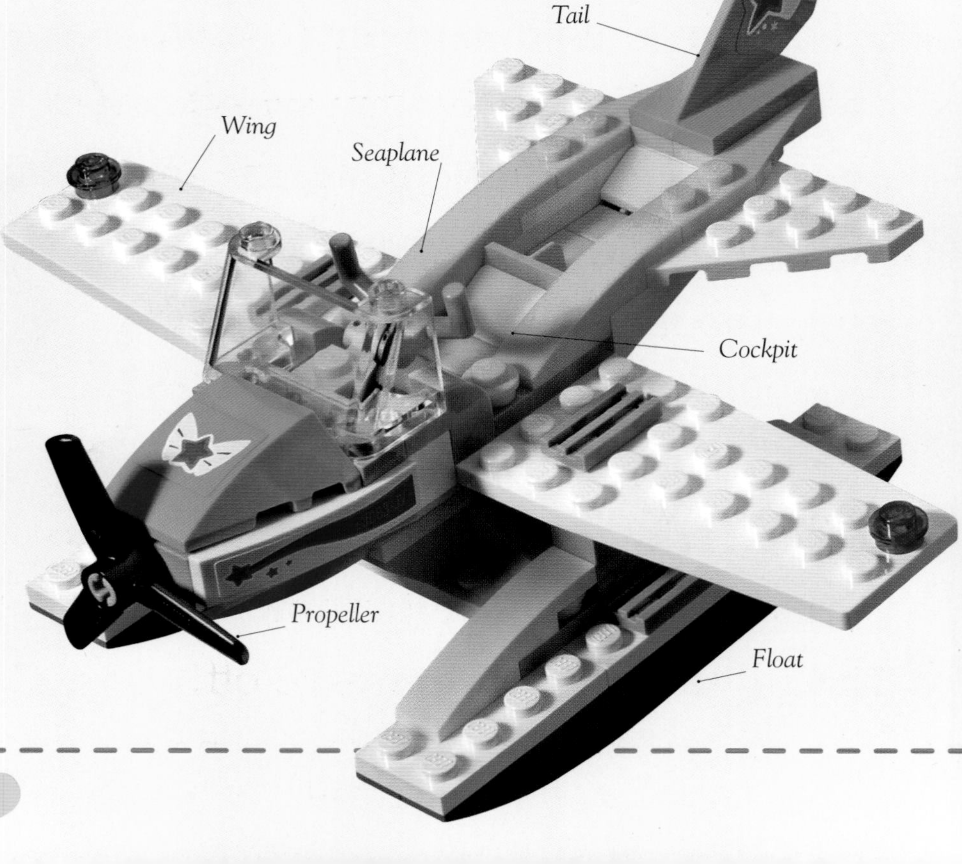

Stephanie is the newest—and youngest—member of the Heartlake City Flying Club.

At last, Stephanie is qualified to fly her seaplane all by herself. However, before she can set off on an exciting flying adventure, she must do some important safety checks. First she must check the weather forecast—flying in bad weather would not be fun. Next, she must plan her route and make sure she has enough fuel for the journey. Finally, Stephanie is ready for take off!

After a smooth take off, Stephanie is up, up, and away! The weather is perfect and Stephanie can see for miles. She is going to fly all around Heartlake City and see what her friends are doing.

Look! There's Mia. She's at the stables grooming her horse Bella. Is that Emma over there?

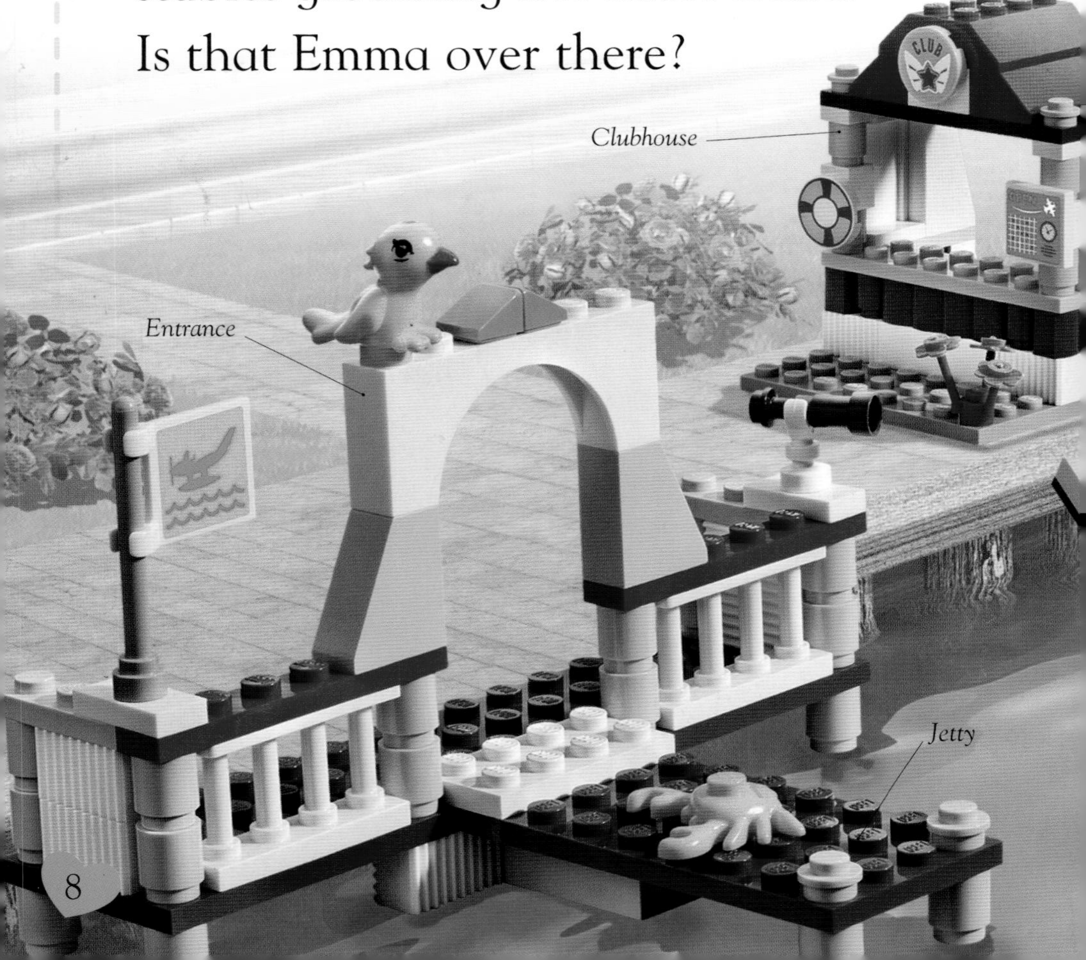

Yes, she's shopping on Main Street. Now Stephanie is flying over Olivia's house; Olivia is building something amazing in the backyard. Stephanie knows just where to find Andrea: There she is, hard at work in the City Park Café. What a great trip! Now it's time for Stephanie to head back and make the perfect landing.

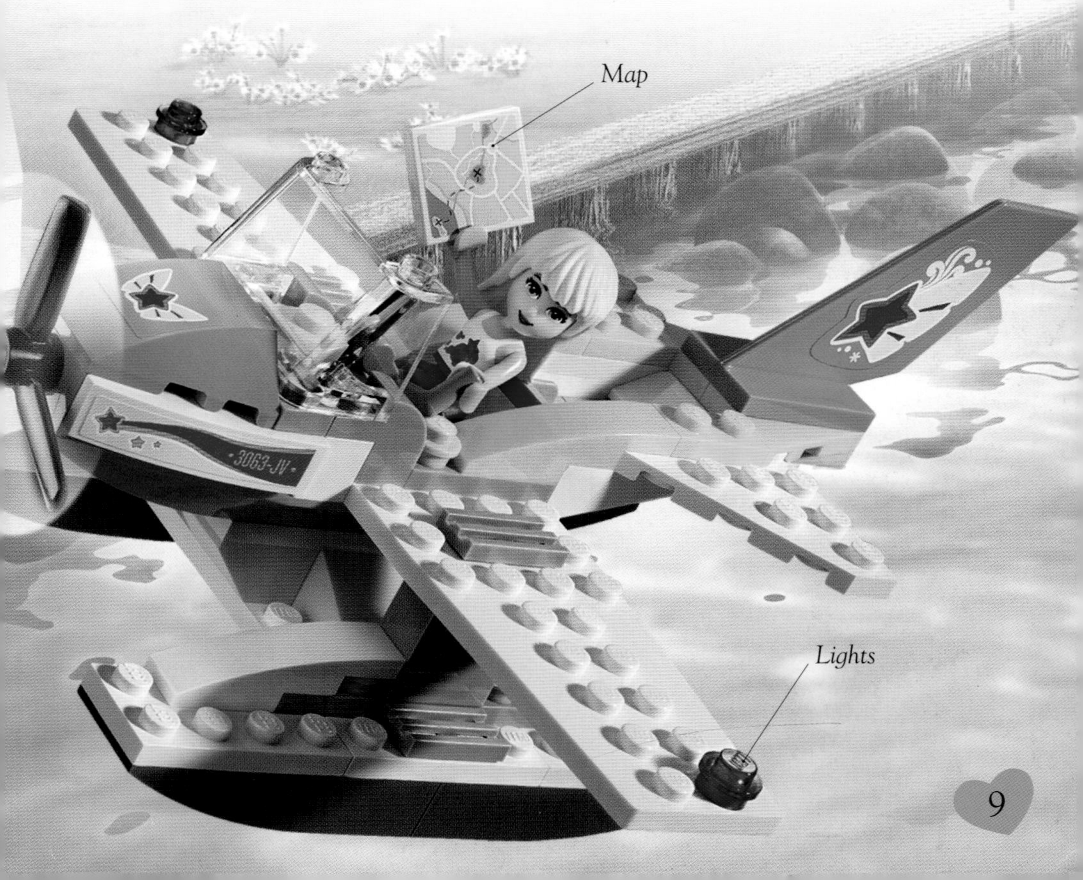

√ Take a trip

Olivia thinks summer is the perfect time to take a trip in her camper van. She loves to explore the countryside around Heartlake City in the stylish pink van. It has a TV in the back and enough space for two people to sleep in it. Olivia knows just who she wants to share this summer adventure with—her friend, Nicole.

Camper van

Gal pals

Olivia and Nicole used to live in the same town, before Olivia moved to Heartlake City. They are good friends and meet up as often as they can.

Olivia calls Nicole and tells her about her plan. Nicole thinks it sounds like fun! The two girls pack their bags and load their bikes and surfboards into the trailer. It's time to set off on their summer adventure!

Olivia has found a quiet spot to park the camper van, so the two friends set off on a bike ride. It's good exercise, and a great way to catch up. The two girls talk about everything that has happened since they last saw each other. Nicole has a new pet cat and has been taking cookery lessons.

Nicole is a very good cook. Grilled chicken is her specialty and Olivia can't wait to try it!

Olivia tells Nicole about her new friends Mia, Stephanie, Andrea, and Emma. Nicole thinks they sound like a lot of fun and would like to meet them all one day.

Back at their camp site, Olivia and Nicole are hungry after a long bike ride. While Olivia prepares a salad, Nicole cooks some chicken on the grill. What a great day!

After a great night's sleep in the camper van, Olivia and Nicole are ready for the next part of their adventure. Olivia drives them to the beach. The girls prepare a delicious picnic and then head down to the ocean with their surfboards.

Picnic basket

The camper van has all the comforts of home, including a TV. It means that the girls won't miss their favorite shows while they're away.

The surf's up and the girls are ready to catch some waves. Nicole has never been surfing before, so Olivia shows her how to do it. After a few wipeouts, Nicole is an expert surfer.

The girls feel quite tired after a day of surfing so they decide to spend the evening relaxing in the van. They play games and watch TV. Tomorrow they will head back home. It's been a wonderful summer adventure!

Surfboard

Find the beat

Mia wants to learn a new skill this summer, so she is teaching herself how to play the drums. She has a cool set of drums and plans to play them every day in her bedroom.

Music fans

Andrea is a music fan, too. She likes to spend her time writing songs and practicing for her next concert.

Radio

Mia likes to practice by turning the radio up high and keeping the beat to her favorite songs. She's getting pretty good at it and is thinking about starting her own rock group. Her new hobby is very cool, but very, very loud.

Mia's parents are pleased that she is interested in music, but they prefer her to practice when they're out!

Summer job

For Andrea, the summer is about working hard and saving money for the future. She works as a waitress at the City Park Café. She takes orders from the customers and then serves them delicious cakes and refreshing drinks. It's hard work, but Andrea doesn't mind because she's saving up for extra singing lessons.

Café owner

Marie owns the City Park Café and bakes all the cakes. She is famous for her yummy cupcakes and mouthwatering pies.

After a hard day at work, Andrea is ready to relax and rest her tired feet. And she knows the perfect way to chill out—by sharing a milkshake with her friends at the City Park Café!

Emma and Mia join Andrea for a milkshake and a slice of one of Marie's famous pies.

Writing adventures

Stephanie is very sociable and she has many friends all over the world. It's a lot of work keeping in touch with all of them, but if anyone can do it, it's super-organized Stephanie! She loves to write long letters to her pen pals.

Pen pal

One of Stephanie's best pen friends is Ella. The two girls write to each other every week and see each other every summer vacation.

Stephanie has designed her own notepaper and she writes all about her adventures with Mia, Emma, Olivia, and Andrea in Heartlake City. Today, Stephanie is posting a letter to her friend Ella asking her if she wants to come to riding camp with Emma and her this summer.

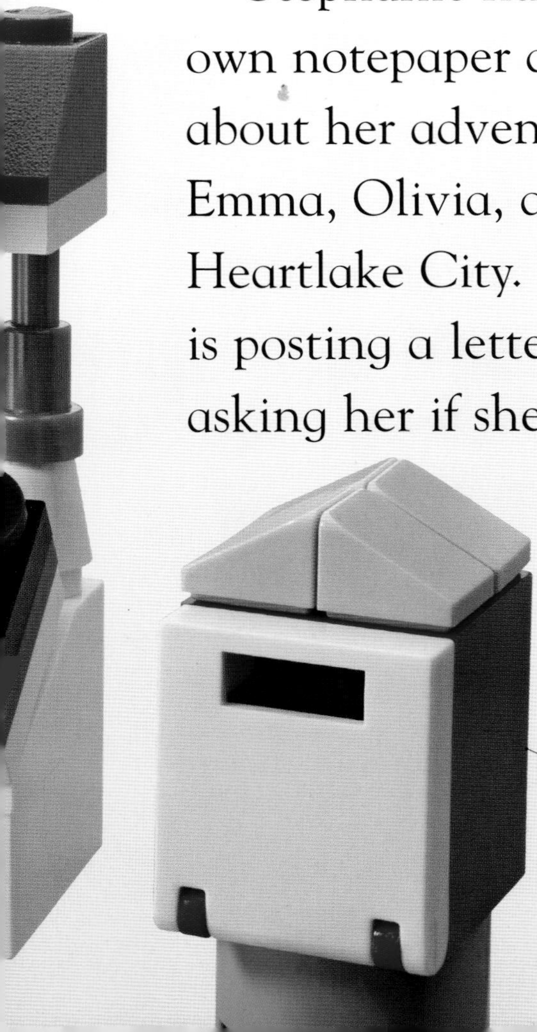

Letterbox

Beach time

When she isn't working at the City Park Café or practicing her singing, Andrea heads to the beach. There's always something fabulous to do there!

If Andrea wants to take it easy, she can just relax and read her favorite book. But if she's looking for adventures, she can go snorkeling and discover the amazing ocean world or search for exciting treasure buried beneath the sandy beach.

Andrea also loves building sandcastles. Her friend Olivia has been teaching her how to construct the most spectacular castles, featuring towers, a moat, and a flag on top. Of course, no matter how well Andrea builds them, her pretty creations are always washed away by the ocean!

Time to relax

Emma thinks that summer isn't all about having exciting adventures. She likes to relax and take it easy after working so hard at school.

Her friends agree and they like to make time to just chill out together.

Emma also has a splash pool in her backyard. It's perfect for taking a dip on a hot summer day.

Emma's summer house is right by the beach. It's the perfect place for Emma, Mia, Stephanie, Olivia, and Andrea to hang out, sunbathe, and catch up on each other's summer adventures. Relaxing in the sun can give the girls a healthy appetite, but they have the perfect snack—ice cream sundaes. They're cool, creamy, and completely delicious!

Outdoor adventures

Mia and Olivia agree that summer is no time to be stuck inside all the time. The weather is always good in Heartlake City so they both like to have exciting outdoor adventures.

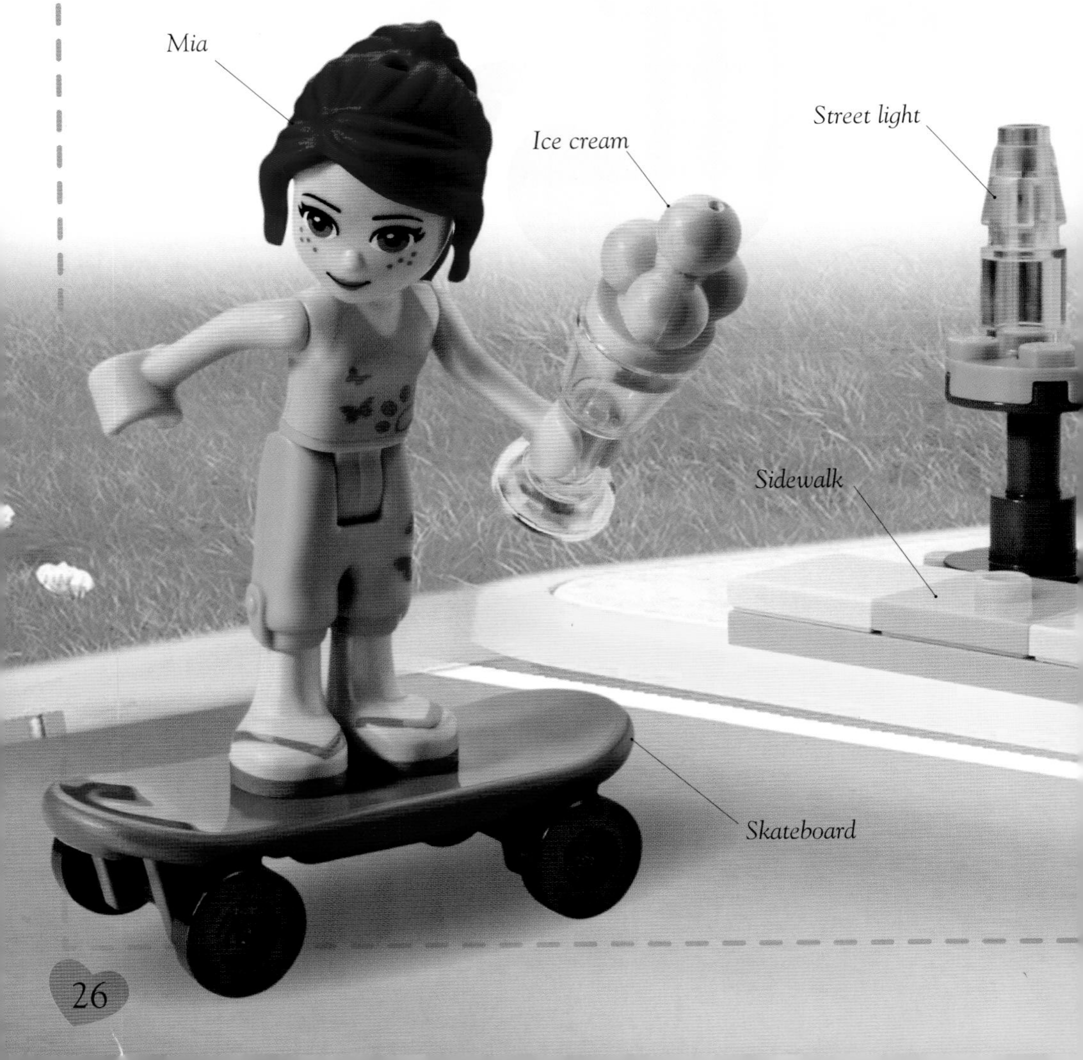

Olivia prefers speedboats to skateboards. She has learned to drive her parents' speedboat and she loves to take it out on the ocean.

Mia's favorite outdoor pastime is skateboarding. She spends a lot of time at the City Park practicing jumps and tricks. Soon she thinks she'll be ready to enter a local skateboarding competition.

Skateboarding is also a great way of getting around—it's much quicker than walking! In fact, Mia is so good at skateboarding that she can skate and eat an ice cream at the same time. It's not as easy as it looks!

Indoor adventures

During the summer, Emma tries to spend as much time as possible in her studio. She wants to be a fashion designer so she's already working on her own fashion collection.

Emma thinks her latest creation would look fabulous on Mia!

Laptop

Emma has so many great ideas! In her studio, she uses the internet to research styles and fabrics, then she draws her designs and pins them up on her mood board. She likes to take pictures of all her ideas. Emma takes fashion very seriously and she believes that accessories can make or break an outfit. Well, that's what she's always telling her friends!

Inventing adventures

Olivia is a budding inventor. She has her own workshop where she experiments with new ideas and designs amazing gadgets. This summer she has created her most ambitious invention yet—a robot! His name is Zobo.

Sometimes Olivia is so busy with her inventions that she forgets to go out and have fun with Emma, Andrea, Mia, and Stephanie.

Olivia thinks Zobo is really cool. She can make him fetch things, using her remote control pad. He is really easy to look after, too. Unlike a pet, he doesn't need walking or feeding, all he needs is regular oiling to make sure he doesn't go rusty.

Oil can

Horsing around

Mia, Emma, and Stephanie all agree that summer is perfect for spending more time with their favorite animals—horses. During the summer Mia spends as much time as possible at the stables, grooming, feeding, and riding her horse, Bella.

The riding instructor, Theresa, teaches Emma and Stephanie how to groom horses.

This summer, Stephanie and Emma are going to riding camp, with Stephanie's friend Ella. At riding camp the girls can spend all day with horses. In the morning they have lessons with Theresa, who teaches them how to care for horses.
In the afternoon they can practice riding in the training paddock or go out for longer rides in the countryside. At the end of the day, the girls must groom and feed the horses and then put them safely in their stables.

Helping out

Mia is crazy about all animals, not just horses. During the summer, she is a volunteer helper with the Heartlake City vet. Mia does whatever the vet needs her to. She feeds the animals, cleans their cages, exercises them, and sometimes she just talks to them if they are scared or hurt. Mia loves taking care of animals and they seem to like her, too. She thinks she might like to be a vet one day.

Mia knows it is hard work, but she wants to learn as much as possible from Sophie the vet.

Pet transporter

Animal expert

Sophie the vet is Olivia's aunt. She is trained to treat sick and injured pets and wild animals.

Furry friends

During the summer, Andrea and Mia have more free time to spend with their pets. They think that animals need summer adventures, too! Andrea decides that her rabbit deserves star treatment so she builds him a fabulous new living space.

Mia thinks that her puppy, Charlie, needs a summer makeover. She washes and grooms him, and completes the look with a cute pink bow!

The rabbit's new home has an outside area so he can hop around and get plenty of exercise, and an indoor area with a roof so he can stay warm and dry at night. He also has a special water bottle so he will never be thirsty and Andrea makes sure he is well fed with tasty carrots. What a lucky rabbit! He is a very happy bunny.

Makeover time

Emma thinks that Mia's puppy isn't the only one who deserves a makeover. She wants a new look for summer so she goes to the Butterfly Beauty Shop and asks Sarah for something fabulous!

Emma is always giving her friends great fashion advice so Mia is pleased to be able to help her out, too.

Sarah knows just what to do, and Emma loves it! Now she just needs to complete her look with a cute hair accessory and the perfect shade of lipstick. Emma can't decide which lipstick will look best so she needs advice from one of her friends. Fortunately, Mia is passing by the Beauty Shop and is happy to help Emma out. Her new look is fabulous!

Summer show

Mia has a busy summer, but she makes sure that her pets have fun, too. She enters her puppy, Charlie, into the annual Heartlake City Dog Show. Mia is determined that he will win a prize for Most Agile Puppy, but it is going to take a lot of hard work and practice.

Charlie and Scarlett receive winners' ribbons. They just happen to match their purple bows perfectly!

Fortunately, Mia is a talented animal trainer and Charlie is very clever. On the day of the competition he performs brilliantly. Charlie is the winner! He wins the special trophy, but Olivia's puppy, Scarlett, takes second place.

Mia is extremely proud of her special puppy.

Summer daytrips

Stephanie and Emma love taking trips in their cars. They're happy to drive their friends wherever they want to go—if they can only agree on a plan!

Everyone has a great idea: Emma would like to take a trip to the mall to check out the latest fashions.

If Stephanie's friends are too busy to go for a drive, she takes her dog instead!

Mia suggests a drive out to the countryside to go on a nature hike, but Andrea wants to go and see her favorite pop group in concert. Olivia thinks there's a Science Fair in the next town, but Stephanie has heard there might be a soccer tournament at the City Park. Olivia finally comes up with a practical solution: They can do all these things, one at a time! The Science Fair first, of course...

Secret place

Olivia believes that she doesn't have to travel far for the best summer adventures. That's because she and her friends have an amazing treehouse, which no one else knows about. Olivia found the treehouse near her new house when she moved to Heartlake City and the girls worked hard together to fix it up and make it the perfect meeting place. Now it's Olivia, Andrea, Mia, Emma, and Stephanie's own private space.

Telescope
Olivia built a telescope so the girls can check whether anyone is approaching the treehouse.

At the treehouse the girls can hang out, share their secrets, and plan their next adventure.

Amazing adventures

Emma, Stephanie, Mia, Andrea, and Olivia have had lots of fantastic summer adventures—some relaxing, some thrilling, and some downright hard work! However, they all know what the most important part of any summer adventure is—sharing it with your best friends.

Summer is nearly over but the girls have time for one last barbecue at Olivia's house.

Winter adventures

Soon it will be time for some winter adventures. For Emma that means one thing—snow! She loves winter sports, such as skiing.

Friends can make a good summer, a fabulous summer. Now it's your turn: How will you spend your summer adventure? Who will you share it with?

Quiz

1. What kind of plane does Stephanie fly?

2. Name Olivia's old friend who takes a trip with her.

3. What is Mia's new hobby?

4. What is Andrea's job?

5. Who does Emma think her latest design will look fabulous on?

6. What is the most important part of any summer adventure?

1. A seaplane 2. Nicole 3. Playing the drums 4. A waitress at the Heartlake City Café 5. Mia 6. Your best friends